THE PYTHON PATHFINDER: A COMPREHENSIVE CODING GUIDE

Contents

4

8

1. Prologue to Python

1.1 What is Python?

markdown Copy code: An introduction to Python as an interpreted, high-level programming language.
 - Python's plan reasoning and accentuation on clarity.
 - Use cases and utilizations of Python in different areas.

1.2 Python's Set of experiences

markdown
Duplicate code
 - Brief history of Python's turn of events.
 - Key achievements and adaptations.
 - The job of Python in the programming scene.

1.3 Introducing Python

vbnet

Duplicate code

 - Bit by bit guide on the most proficient method to introduce Python on various working frameworks.

 - An overview of Python distributions like CPython and Anaconda

 - Confirming the establishment and setting up the advancement climate.

1.4 Python Intelligent Shell

markdown

Duplicate code

 - Prologue to the Python intelligent shell (REPL).

 - Fundamental orders and elements of the intuitive shell.

- Involving the intuitive shell for speedy code testing and investigation.

1.5 Composing Your Most memorable Python Program

css

Duplicate code

- A straightforward "Hi, World!" program.

- Making sense of the design of a Python script.

- Running Python scripts from the order line.

1.6 Figuring out Python Language structure

markdown

Duplicate code

- Essential language structure rules in Python (space, colons, and so on.).

- Outline of Python's dynamic composing.

- Remarking and recording code in Python.

1.7 Python Data Types

Markdown Copy Code:

An Overview of the Basic Data Types (Integers, Floats, Strings, and Booleans)

- Dynamic composing and variable task.

- Fundamental procedure on information types.

1.8 Normal Python Worked in Capabilities

slam

Duplicate code

- Outline of ordinarily utilized worked in capabilities (print, len, type, and so on.).

- Models delineating the use of these capabilities.

- Presenting the Python documentation as an important asset.

This extended presentation ought to give a strong groundwork to fledglings to Python, covering fundamental viewpoints from establishment to essential programming ideas. You can additionally expound on each subtopic depending on the situation, consolidating straightforward models and activities to build up learning.

2. Getting everything rolling

2.1 Composing Your Most memorable Python Program

graphql
Duplicate code
 - Expanding on the "Hi, World!" guide to incorporate client input.
 -          Investigating   print proclamations,   factors,   and fundamental   number-crunching tasks.
 - Accentuating the significance of testing and making changes.

2.2 Grasping Python Punctuation

markdown
Duplicate code
 - Digging further into Python's space and block structure.
 - Making sense of the meaning of colons and whitespace in Python.

- Presenting the idea of code blocks and how not entirely settled.

2.3 Variables and Data Types

Markdown Copy code:

Naming conventions and declaring variables

- Investigating various information types in more detail (records, tuples, word references).

- The fundamental manipulations and operations involving variables and data types.

2.4 Client Info and Result

sql

Duplicate code

- Utilizing the 'input()' capability to get client input.

- Designing result with the 'print()' capability.

- Converting data types and handling user input

2.5 Administrators and Articulations

markdown
Duplicate code
 - Outline of math, correlation, and sensible administrators.
 -   Building articulations and figuring out the request for tasks.
 -   Involving administrators in restrictive explanations and circles.

2.6 Control Stream

markdown
Duplicate code
 - Prologue to decision-production with 'if', 'else', and 'elif' articulations.
 - Using for and while loops to create loops
 - Models showing the progression of control in Python programs.

2.7 Troubleshooting Nuts and bolts

vbnet

Duplicate code

- Normal blunders and how to decipher mistake messages.

- Involving print articulations for troubleshooting.

- An overview of the tools and methods used in debugging

The expanded "Getting Started" section aims to provide a hands-on introduction to Python programming by addressing fundamental ideas like variables, data types, user input, and the fundamental control flow. Each subtopic ought to incorporate useful models and activities to build up learning and support trial and error.

3. Control Stream

3.1 Restrictive Articulations (if, else, elif)

markdown
Duplicate code
 - Understanding the fundamental linguistic structure of the 'if' proclamation.
 - Presenting the 'else' statement for elective execution.
 - Utilizing 'elif' for various contingent branches.
 - Models showing the utilization of contingent explanations in different situations.

3.2 Circles (for, while)

markdown
Duplicate code

- Investigating the 'for' circle for repeating over groupings (records, strings, and so on.).

- Understanding the 'while' circle for endless emphasis.

- Controlling circles with 'break' and 'proceed' explanations.

- Commonsense models exhibiting the utilization of circles in Python programs.

3.3 Control Stream in real life

markdown
Duplicate code

- Making programs that consolidate restrictive articulations and circles.

- Tackling basic issues utilizing control stream develops.

- Underlining the significance of composing lucid and viable code.

3.4 Settled Circles and Conditionals

markdown
Duplicate code
 - Grasping settled circles and their applications.
 - Utilizing settled conditionals for more perplexing independent direction.
 - Best practices for keeping up with clearness in settled structures.
Introducing the "try" and "except" blocks for handling exceptions in the

3.5 Error Handling

with Try and Except Markdown Copy Code section.
 - Utilizing 'else' lastly with 'attempt' and 'aside from'.
 - Illustrations of how to handle errors in actual situations.

3.6 Rundown Understandings

css

Duplicate code

- Prologue to list understandings for succinct and expressive code.

- Using a single line of code to create lists.

- Benefits and use cases for list perceptions.

3.7 Word reference and Set Understandings

css

Duplicate code

- Applying cognizance procedures to word references and sets.

- Making word references and sets in a more smaller structure.

- Pragmatic models exhibiting the utilization of cognizances.

This extended "Control Stream" segment gives an exhaustive outline of fundamental programming develops in Python, including restrictive proclamations, circles, mistake taking care of, and perception procedures. Each subtopic ought to incorporate models and activities to help students practice and assimilate the ideas.

4. Capabilities

4.1 Characterizing Capabilities

slam
Duplicate code

- Grasping the fundamental language structure for characterizing capabilities.
- The significance of capability names and naming shows.
- Function definitions' arguments and parameters.

4.2 Capability Boundaries and Bring Values back

sql
Duplicate code

- Investigating various sorts of capability boundaries (positional, catchphrase).
- Default boundary values for additional adaptable capabilities.

- Returning qualities utilizing the 'return' proclamation.

4.3 Extension and Lifetime of Factors

sql
Duplicate code

- Figuring out factor scope (neighborhood and worldwide).
- The life expectancy of factors inside and outside capabilities.
- The most effective methods for naming variables and avoiding naming conflicts.

4.4 Recursion in Bash: Copying Code: An Overview of Recursive Functions

- Grasping the base case and recursive case.
- Models exhibiting recursion in taking care of issues.

4.5 Lambda Capabilities

slam
Duplicate code

- Outline of unknown capabilities utilizing 'lambda'.
- Use cases for lambda capabilities and their sentence structure.
- Standing out lambda capabilities from standard named capabilities.

4.6 Higher-Request Capabilities

slam
Duplicate code

- Grasping capabilities as top of the line residents.
- Passing capabilities as contentions to different capabilities.
- Returning capabilities from different capabilities.

4.7 Capability Decorators

markdown
Duplicate code

- Prologue to decorators for changing or expanding capabilities.

- Making and using straightforward decorators.

- Normal use cases for decorators in Python.

4.8 Modules and Modular Programming Markdown code

copying is the process of organizing code into modules to make it easier to maintain.

- Bringing in and involving modules in Python.

- Making your own modules and sorting out capabilities.

This extended "Capabilities" segment expects to give a strong comprehension of capabilities in Python, covering the nuts and bolts of capability definition, boundaries, and return values, as well as further developed subjects like recursion, lambda capabilities, and decorators.

Each subtopic ought to incorporate models and activities to build up the ideas and energize involved practice.

5. Information Designs

5.1 Records

vbnet
Duplicate code

- Prologue to records as requested, alterable assortments.

- Essential procedure on records (ordering, cutting, annexing, adjusting).

- Using loops to iterate over lists.

5.2 Tuples in Markdown Copy Code:

Understanding tuples as collections that are ordered and cannot be changed

- Use cases for tuples and the benefits they provide.

- Working with tuple methods and unpacking tuples

5.3 Word references

markdown
Duplicate code
 - Outline of word references as key-esteem matches.
 - Creating, modifying, and gaining access to dictionary components.
 - Emphasizing over keys, values, and things in word references.

5.4 Sets

sql
Duplicate code
 - Prologue to sets as unordered, extraordinary assortments.
 - Operations on sets (union, intersection, and difference).
 - Viable utilizations of sets in Python.

5.5 Further developed Rundown Tasks

markdown
Duplicate code

- List perception for brief rundown creation.

- Involving the 'count' capability for cycle with files.

- Applying 'speed' for consolidating various iterables.

5.6 Working with Settled Information Designs

markdown
Duplicate code

- Making and controlling arrangements of records.

- Settling word references and sets for additional intricate information structures.

- Viable models exhibiting the utilization of settled structures.

5.7 Picking the Right Information Construction

markdown
Duplicate code
 - Rules for choosing the proper information structure.
 - Understanding the compromises between records, tuples, word references, and sets.
 - True instances of information structure determination.

5.8 Prologue to NumPy (Discretionary)

markdown
Duplicate code
 - Outline of NumPy for mathematical figuring in Python.
 - Making and controlling NumPy exhibits.

- Fundamental activities and capabilities given by NumPy.

This extended "Information Designs" segment expects to cover essential information structures in Python, giving viable bits of knowledge into their utilization and applications. Each subtopic ought to remember hands-for models and activities to support understanding and empower trial and error with various information structures.

6. Record Dealing with

6.1 Perusing from Records

scss

Duplicate code

 - Prologue to record dealing with in Python.

 - Opening and shutting records utilizing 'open()' and 'close()' capabilities.

 - Using read() and readline() to read lines as well as entire files.

6.2 Composition to Documents

markdown

Duplicate code

 - Making and writing to new documents.

 - Annexing information to existing documents.

 - Utilizing the 'compose()' technique and the 'with'

proclamation for programmed record conclusion.

6.3 Working with Record Articles

markdown
Duplicate code

- Understanding record objects and their techniques ('read', 'compose', 'look for', 'tell').

- Exploring through a document with the 'look for()' strategy.

- Recovering the ongoing situation in the record with 'tell()'.

6.4 Dealing with Special cases in Record I/O

vbnet
Duplicate code

- Managing potential mistakes while working with documents.

- Involving attempt with the exception of blocks for vigorous document taking care of.

- Guaranteeing appropriate record conclusion with the 'at last' block.

6.5 Working with Various File Formats Markdown Copy Code –
Working with text files (.txt)

- An overview of how to handle CSV (Comma-Separated Values) files.

- Prologue to JSON (JavaScript Item Documentation) record dealing with.

6.6 Working with Double Records (Discretionary)

sql
Duplicate code

- Understanding double record taking care of.

- Using the "rb" and "wb" modes to read and write binary files

- Managing twofold information and byte control.

6.7 CSV and Succeed Handling with pandas (Discretionary)

markdown
Duplicate code

- Prologue to the pandas library for information control.

- Perusing and composing CSV documents utilizing pandas DataFrames.

- Essential Succeed document handling with pandas.

6.8 Best Practices for Handling Files Markdown Copy code –

Closing files correctly and utilizing the "with" statement

- Techniques for dealing with errors during file operations

- Picking the right document design for explicit use cases.

This extended "Document Taking care of" segment gives a thorough manual for perusing from and writing to records in Python. It covers fundamental record activities, working with various document designs, mistake taking care of, and discretionary segments on parallel records and pandas for cutting edge document handling. Each subtopic ought to incorporate models and activities to assist students with acquiring pragmatic involvement with document taking care of.

7. Error Handling

7.1 Understanding Exceptions Markdown Copy Code:

An explanation of Python's exceptions

- Normal sorts of special cases and their implications.

- The significance of taking care of special cases for powerful projects.

7.2 try and except Blocks markdown Copy code –

How to use the "try" and "except" blocks and their syntax

- Taking care of explicit special cases with various 'aside from' blocks.

- Utilizing a general 'with the exception of' block and catching the exemption object.

7.3 Handling Multiple Exceptions
Markdown Copy code:

Using a single "except" block to handle multiple exceptions.

- Utilizing tuple sentence structure to get numerous special cases.

- Requesting and putting together numerous 'with the exception of' blocks.

7.4 at long last Block

markdown
Duplicate code

- Presenting the 'at long last' block for code that ought to constantly execute.

- Use cases for the 'at last' block in asset the executives.

- Consolidating 'attempt', 'aside from', lastly for thorough mistake dealing with.

7.5 Raising Special cases

markdown
Duplicate code

- Expressly raising exemptions utilizing the 'raise' articulation.

- Making custom exemption classes for particular mistake dealing with.

- Controlling system stream with raised special cases.

7.6 Exceptions in Functions:

Strategies for Handling Exceptions in Functions Markdown Copy Code

- Spreading out errors to the code that is calling them.

- Including "try," "except," and "finally" in the definitions of functions.

7.7 Exemption Binding and Tracebacks

lua
Duplicate code

- Understanding the traceback and how it helps in troubleshooting.

- Binding special cases for a more useful blunder report.

- Utilizing the 'traceback' module for cutting edge exemption dealing with.

7.8 Normal Blunders and Troubleshooting

markdown
Duplicate code
- Recognizing and tending to normal blunders in Python.

- Troubleshooting procedures utilizing print articulations and investigating apparatuses.

- Prologue to Python troubleshooting devices (e.g., pdb).

This extended "Blunder Dealing with" segment gives a careful investigation of dealing with exemptions in Python, covering central ideas like attempt, with the exception of, lastly hinders, as well as further developed subjects like raising special cases, taking care of exemptions in capabilities, and viable troubleshooting methods. Each subtopic ought to incorporate models and activities to build up understanding and viable application.

8. Object-Arranged Programming (OOP)

8.1 Classes and Items

markdown
Duplicate code
 - Prologue to classes and items as basic OOP ideas.
 -    Characterizing classes and making occurrences (objects).
 -    Understanding a class's characteristics and methods.

8.2 Qualities and Techniques

kotlin
Duplicate code
 - Investigating example ascribes and class credits.
 - Characterizing techniques inside a class and figuring out self.
 - Access modifiers (public, private, secured) in Python.

8.3 Legacy

markdown
Duplicate code

- Grasping the idea of legacy in OOP.

- Making subclasses and acquiring ascribes and strategies.

- Superseding strategies in a subclass.

8.4 Epitome

vbnet
Duplicate code

- Prologue to epitome for information stowing away and insurance.

- Making private ascribes and strategies utilizing naming shows.

- Involving property strategies for controlled quality access.

8.5 Polymorphism

markdown
Duplicate code

- Outline of polymorphism and its advantages in OOP.

- Accomplishing polymorphism through strategy over-burdening and abrogating.

- Executing polymorphism with theoretical classes and points of interaction.

8.6 Class Constructors and Destructors Markdown Copy Code:

Recognizing the "_init_" method as a constructor

- The job of the '_del_' technique as a destructor.

- Introduction and cleanup processes in classes.

8.7 Class Methods and Static Methods vbnet Copy code:

How to tell instance methods, class methods, and static methods apart

- Characterizing and utilizing class techniques and static strategies.

- Use cases for each sort of technique.

8.8 Organization and Conglomeration

markdown
Duplicate code

- Grasping arrangement and accumulation as options in contrast to legacy.

- Making complex articles through creation.

- Consolidating objects through collection.

A comprehensive guide to OOP principles in Python can be found in this expanded "Object-Oriented

Programming (OOP)" section. It covers the fundamentals of classes and articles, investigates key OOP ideas like legacy and embodiment, and presents progressed subjects like polymorphism and creation. Each subtopic ought to incorporate models and activities to assist students with acquiring active involvement in OOP ideas in Python.

9. Modules and Libraries

9.1 Bringing in Modules

markdown
Duplicate code
 - Figuring out the idea of modules in Python.
 - Bringing in worked in modules and utilizing their functionalities.
 - Making and bringing in client characterized modules.

9.2 Module Associating and Namespaces

javascript
Duplicate code
 - Making nom de plumes for modules with the 'as' catchphrase.
 - Understanding module namespaces and trying not to name clashes.

- Best practices for module association and naming.

9.3 Investigating Worked in Modules

markdown
Duplicate code

- Outline of normally utilized worked in modules (e.g., 'math', 'irregular').

- Investigating modules for document taking care of ('os', 'shutil').

- Utilizing the 'datetime' module for working with dates and times.

9.4 Packages in Python:

Creating and Using Packages in SQL Copy Code Understanding the Packages concept in Python

- Putting together modules into bundles for better undertaking structure.

- Bringing in and utilizing modules from inside bundles.

9.5 Outsider Libraries and Establishment

markdown
Duplicate code

- Prologue to the Python Bundle List (PyPI).
- Introducing outsider libraries utilizing 'pip'.
- Investigating well known libraries like NumPy, Pandas, and Solicitations.

9.6 NumPy for Mathematical Figuring

markdown
Duplicate code

- Outline of the NumPy library for proficient mathematical activities.
- Making and controlling NumPy exhibits.

- Fundamental numerical tasks and works given by NumPy.

9.7 Pandas for Information Investigation

markdown
Duplicate code

- Prologue to the Pandas library for information control and investigation.
- Utilizing DataFrames and Pandas Series.
- Stacking and cleaning information utilizing Pandas.

9.8 Solicitations for HTTP Dealing with

markdown
Duplicate code

- Involving the Solicitations library for making HTTP demands.
- Sending GET and POST demands and taking care of reactions.

- Essential mistake endlessly taking care of JSON reactions.

This extended "Modules and Libraries" segment covers the fundamentals of working with modules, investigates famous underlying modules, and presents key outsider libraries for different purposes. Each subtopic ought to incorporate models and activities to assist students with acquiring functional involvement with using modules and libraries in Python.

10. Working with APIs

10.1 Grasping APIs

markdown
Duplicate code
-    Prologue to Application Programming Points of interaction (APIs).
 - Outline of Relaxing APIs and their significance.
 - Making sense of Programming interface endpoints, solicitations, and reactions.

10.2 Making Programming interface Solicitations with Python

vbnet
Duplicate code
 - Utilizing the 'demands' library to make HTTP demands.

- Sending GET solicitations to recover information from a Programming interface.
- Taking care of question boundaries and headers in Programming interface demands.

10.3 Parsing JSON Reactions

javascript
Duplicate code
- Outline of JSON (JavaScript Article Documentation) design.
- Parsing JSON reactions from Programming interface demands.
- Extricating and controlling information from JSON structures.

10.4 Verification with APIs

markdown
Duplicate code
- Figuring out verification techniques (e.g., Programming interface keys, OAuth).

- Remembering verification boundaries for Programming interface demands.

- Dealing with access tokens and invigorate tokens.

10.5 Mistake Taking care of in Programming interface Solicitations

vbnet

Duplicate code

- Managing normal mistakes in Programming interface reactions.

- Utilizing status codes to recognize achievement or disappointment.

- Carrying out vigorous blunder dealing with in Programming interface cooperations.

10.6 Rate Limiting and Throttling Markdown Copy Code:

Getting a handle on API rate limits and throttling.

- Taking care of rate-restricting limitations in Programming interface demands.

- Methods for maximizing performance and avoiding API rate caps.

10.7 Working with Public APIs

vbnet

Duplicate code

- Investigating well known public APIs (e.g., OpenWeatherMap, GitHub).

- Making requests for real-world data to public APIs.

- Building straightforward applications utilizing public APIs.

10.8 Structure Your Programming interface Client (Discretionary)

vbnet

Duplicate code

- Making a straightforward Python class for collaborating with a particular Programming interface.

-     Epitomizing Programming interface usefulness inside a custom class.

- Best practices for designing API clients that can be reused

A comprehensive tutorial on how to use Python to interact with APIs can be found in the expanded "Working with APIs" section. It covers the essentials of making Programming interface demands, taking care of reactions, verification, blunder dealing with, and working with public APIs. Each subtopic ought to incorporate models and activities to assist students with acquiring involved insight in using APIs with Python.

11. Web Improvement Fundamentals

11.1 Prologue to Web Improvement

markdown
Duplicate code
 - Outline of web improvement and its parts.
 - Figuring out the client-server model.
 - Nuts and bolts of HTTP and how it works with correspondence on the web.

11.2 Introduction to HTML (Hypertext Markup Language)

css Copy code as the standard markup language for web pages
 - Making an essential HTML report structure.
 - Understanding HTML labels, components, and properties.

11.3 CSS (Flowing Templates)

css

Duplicate code

- Outline of CSS for styling and designing HTML archives.

- Applying styles to HTML components utilizing CSS.

- Figuring out selectors, properties, and values in CSS.

11.4 css Copy code: An introduction to JavaScript as a client-side scripting language for web development

- Composing basic JavaScript code inside HTML reports.

- Cooperating with HTML components utilizing JavaScript.

11.5 Markdown Copy Code for Responsive Web Design:

Recognizing the significance of responsive design

- Utilizing media inquiries to make responsive designs.

- Creating web pages that can be viewed on a variety of screen sizes.

11.6 Prologue to Front-End Systems (e.g., Bootstrap)

markdown
Duplicate code

- Outline of front-end systems for proficient web advancement.

- Prologue to Bootstrap and its lattice framework.

- Building responsive and outwardly engaging pages with Bootstrap.

11.7 Fundamental Web Structures

css
Duplicate code

- Making HTML structures for client input.

- Understanding structure components like information fields, fastens, and names.

- Utilizing JavaScript and HTML to handle form submissions.

11.8 Prologue to Back-End Improvement (Discretionary)

vbnet

Duplicate code

- Outline of back-end improvement and its part in web applications.

- Prologue to server-side programming dialects (e.g., Python with Cup).

- Nuts and bolts of dealing with solicitations and reactions on the server.

11.9 Web Development Tools and Workflow Markdown Copy Code:

An Overview of Browser-Based Developer Tools

 - Utilizing version control systems for web development, such as Git.

 - The fundamentals of deploying a basic web application.

This extended "Web Improvement Rudiments" segment covers the primary parts of web advancement, including HTML, CSS, JavaScript, responsive plan, and early on ideas of both front-end and back-end advancement. Each subtopic ought to incorporate models and activities to help students practice and apply their insight in building fundamental pages and applications.

12. Form Control with Git

12.1 Prologue to Form Control

markdown
Duplicate code

 - Understanding the requirement for adaptation control in programming advancement.
 - Advantages of rendition control, joint effort, and following changes.
 - Outline of dispersed form control frameworks.

12.2 Installing and configuring user settings for Git markdown Copy code:

 Getting Started

 - Instating a Git store for another venture.
 - Essential Git orders: 'git add', 'git commit', 'git status'.

12.3 Git Stretching and Blending

markdown
Duplicate code
 - Making branches for equal turn of events.
 - Utilizing "git checkout" to switch between branches.
 - Resolving conflicts and merging branches with "git merge."

12.4 Working with Distant Stores

javascript
Duplicate code
 - Adding a distant store with 'git remote'.
 - Cloning a store with 'git clone'.
 - Pushing changes to a far off store with 'git push'.

12.5 Pulling Changes and Dealing with Clashes

javascript
Duplicate code

- Getting changes from a distant store with 'git bring'.

- Pulling changes from a distant vault with 'git pull'.

- Settling combine clashes and grasping struggle markers.

12.6 Git Log and History Investigation

slam
Duplicate code

- Seeing commit history with 'git log'.

- Exploring and investigating changes in the commit history.

- Separating and designing log yield for lucidness.

12.7 Labeling and Deliveries

sql
Duplicate code
 - Making labels for explicit places in the commit history.
 - Forming discharges with labels.
 - Posting and erasing labels with Git.

12.8 Cooperative Work processes with Git

markdown
Duplicate code
 - Cooperative improvement utilizing branches.
 - Pull demands and code surveys in a cooperative climate.
 - Overseeing highlight branches and bug fixes.

12.9 Git Best Practices

markdown
Duplicate code
 - Committing much of the time and composing significant commit messages.
 - Keeping commits centered and staying away from pointless changes.
 - Overlooking records and registries with '.gitignore'.
This extended "Variant Control with Git" segment gives a far reaching manual for involving Git for rendition control in programming improvement. It covers the essentials of Git orders, spreading, blending, distant stores, joint effort, and best practices. Each subtopic ought to incorporate models and activities to assist students with acquiring viable involvement with

involving Git for dealing with their undertakings.

13. Best Practices and Tips

13.1 Code Style and Energy 8

css
Duplicate code
-      Complying   with   Python
Improvement Proposition 8 (Kick
8) rules.
 - Reliable space, naming shows,
and code design.
 - Utilizing apparatuses like linters
to authorize code style.

13.2 Composing Perfect and Coherent Code

markdown
Duplicate code
 - Focusing on meaningfulness over
shrewdness.

- Remarking sensibly and involving docstrings for documentation.

- Condensing difficult tasks into more manageable, appropriately named functions.

13.3 Productive Troubleshooting Methods

markdown
Duplicate code

- Involving print proclamations for straightforward troubleshooting.

- Using Python's built-in "pdb" debugger to solve more difficult problems.

- Understanding normal mistake messages and traceback data.

13.4 Successful Utilization of Capabilities and Seclusion

vbnet
Duplicate code
 - Keeping capabilities little and zeroed in on a solitary errand.
 - Staying away from worldwide factors whenever the situation allows.
 - Embodying related usefulness into modules.

13.5 Best Practices for Version Control

Markdown Copy code - Regular, meaningful commits with clear messages
 - Making branches for new highlights and bug fixes.
 - Pulling changes routinely and settling clashes speedily.

13.6 Testing Methodologies

markdown
Duplicate code
-   Composing unit tests for capabilities and modules.
-   Understanding test-driven improvement (TDD) standards.
- Making use of frameworks for testing like "unittest" or "pytest."

13.7 Documentation and Remarks

markdown
Duplicate code
- Composing clear and succinct documentation for capabilities and modules.
- Making judicious use of inline comments for clarification.
- Producing documentation with devices like Sphinx.

13.8 Profiling code to find performance

Bottlenecks is part of optimizing code for performance.

- Utilizing fitting information designs and calculations.

- Adjusting lucidness and execution while enhancing.

13.9 Security Considerations Markdown Copy code

- Preventing common security flaws like SQL injection and XSS

- Disinfecting client inputs and approving information.

- Staying up to date on Python security best practices.

13.10 Consistent Learning and Investigation

vbnet

Duplicate code

- Staying up with the latest with Python refreshes and new elements.
- Investigating progressed points and libraries in Python.
- Drawing in with the Python people group through discussions, meetups, and gatherings.

This "Accepted procedures and Tips" segment gives direction on composing spotless, proficient, and viable Python code. Debugging, version control, testing, documentation, performance enhancement, security, and continuous learning are all covered. Each subtopic ought to offer pragmatic counsel and tips to assist students with becoming capable and successful Python designers.

14. Subsequent stages

14.1 High level Themes

vbnet
Duplicate code
 - Investigating progressed Python highlights (decorators, metaclasses).
 - Figuring out simultaneousness and parallelism with strings and multiprocessing.
 - Prologue to nonconcurrent programming with async/anticipate.

14.2 Ventures for Training

markdown
Duplicate code
 - Empowering the improvement of little activities to apply abilities.

- Recommending project thoughts with expanding intricacy.
- Giving assets and direction to project-based learning.

14.3 Adding to Open Source

markdown
Duplicate code

- Outline of open-source advancement and its advantages.
- Finding and adding to open-source Python projects.
- Best practices for working together on GitHub.

14.4 High level Web Advancement (Discretionary)

markdown
Duplicate code

- Extending comprehension of web advancement structures (Django, Carafe).

- Investigating client-side frameworks like Vue, Angular, and React.

- Constructing more complicated web applications.

14.5 Data Science and Machine Learning

(Optional) vbnet Copy code - Data science libraries (NumPy, Pandas) introduction

- Investigating AI with scikit-learn.

- Diving into profound learning with TensorFlow or PyTorch.

14.6 Online protection with Python (Discretionary)

markdown
Duplicate code

- Figuring out Python's part in network protection.

- Investigating instruments for entrance testing and moral hacking.

- Finding out about security mechanization and prearranging.

14.7 Structure APIs with Cup or Django (Discretionary)

.

markdown
Duplicate code

- Making Soothing APIs utilizing Jar or Django.

- Carrying out confirmation and approval.

- ensuring APIs are robust by documenting and testing them.

14.8 DevOps and Automation (Optional)

Copy code in Markdown - An overview of DevOps principles and practices

- Robotizing assignments with apparatuses like Ansible or Texture.

- Implementing continuous deployment and integration.

14.9 Vocation Advancement and Pursuit of employment

markdown
Duplicate code
 - Creating a convincing resume and portfolio.
 - Getting ready for specialized interviews.
 - Investigating open positions in Python improvement.

14.10 Local area Contribution

markdown
Duplicate code
 - Partaking in Python people group and gatherings.
 - Going to nearby meetups and gatherings.
 - Organizing with individual designers for cooperation and learning.

This "Following stages" segment gives a guide to students to proceed with their Python process past the nuts and bolts. It suggests advanced topics, practice projects, open source contributions, and alternate routes into specialized fields like web development, data science, cybersecurity, and DevOps. Furthermore, it offers direction on vocation advancement and local area contribution to encourage consistent learning and expert development.

www.ingramcontent.com/pod-product-compliance
Lightning Source LLC
Chambersburg PA
CBHW050046260726
48658CB00005B/1795